HOW COOL
IS THIS?

DK PUBLISHING

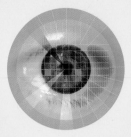

LONDON, NEW YORK
MELBOURNE, MUNICH, and DELHI

Senior editor Wendy Horobin
Project designer Laura Roberts-Jensen
Editors Penny Smith, Fleur Star, Ben Morgan
Designers Sadie Thomas, Pamela Shiels,
Jemma Westing
US editor Margaret Parrish
Picture researcher Myriam Mégharbi
Production editor Andy Hilliard
Production controller Claire Pearson
Jacket designers Karen Hood, Laura Roberts-Jensen
Art director Martin Wilson
Publishing manager Bridget Giles
Creative director Jane Bull
Publisher Mary Ling

Consultant Roger Bridgman

First published in the United States in 2011 by
DK Publishing
375 Hudson Street, New York, New York 10014

11 12 13 14 15 10 9 8 7 6 5 4 3 2 1
001–180693–Aug/11

A catalog record for this book
is available from the Library of Congress.

ISBN: 978-0-7566-8604-8

Printed and bound in China by Hung Hing

Discover more at
www.dk.com

CONTENTS

BUBBLES

BUBBLES ARE AMAZINGLY DELICATE THINGS.

They are made of nothing more than water, soap, and air. As they float, they form a perfect sphere that shimmers with many different colors.

Multicolored bubbles

The surface of a bubble shows a constantly swirling pattern of colors. It has some of the colors you see in a rainbow, as well as magenta, silver, and gold. The colors show how thick the bubble's skin is. When a bubble is almost entirely black, it is very thin and ready to pop.

The turquoise areas are thickest, then blue, magenta, red, and yellow.

Soap story

Soap is what gives the bubble its stretchiness and makes it last. Soap molecules are chains of hydrogen and carbon atoms. One end of the molecule likes water, the other hates it.

The skin of a bubble is like a sandwich. It has two layers of soap molecules with water in-between. The water-loving heads of the soap molecules stick into the water, while the tails stick out into the air.

Colors form when light waves bounce off the inner AND outer walls of a bubble. The waves crash into each other, changing their pattern and therefore the bubble's colors.

Water molecules

Soap molecules

A bubble has three layers.

BUBBLES BURST because they dry out. Despite the soap molecules forming a skin, the water quickly evaporates. Adding a few drops of glycerin to the bubble mix makes them last longer. Bubbles also burst if they touch a dry object, like a finger.

The bubble shatters in an instant, racing rapidly from the point of contact to the opposite side.

As the bubble bursts, it turns back into thousands of tiny droplets of soap mixture.

GLOWSTICK

IF YOU BEND AND SHAKE A GLOWSTICK it will burst into light. Its magical glow is produced by a chemical reaction between two liquids. Many chemical reactions release energy in the form of heat, but this reaction produces nothing but light.

Glowsticks don't get hot so you can hold them in your hand.

What makes a glowstick glow?

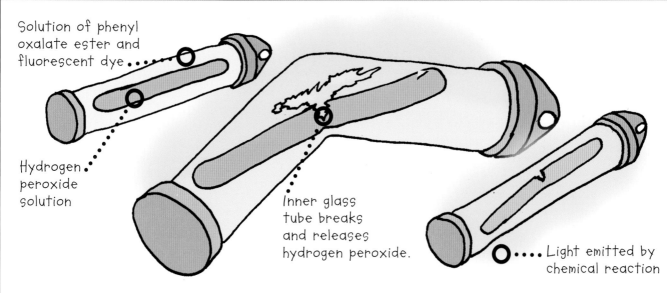

Solution of phenyl oxalate ester and fluorescent dye

Hydrogen peroxide solution

Inner glass tube breaks and releases hydrogen peroxide.

Light emitted by chemical reaction

A glowstick consists of a plastic tube containing a smaller glass tube. Each tube contains a different liquid. When you bend the stick, the glass tube breaks and the two liquids mix. The reaction makes the fluorescent dye give off light.

Putting a glowstick in the refrigerator before use will make the reaction last longer, but give less light. To make it brighter, put it in hot water. The rise in temperature speeds up the chemical reaction, making the light more intense.

FIREFLIES produce light in a similar way to glowsticks, mixing two chemicals inside their tails to create a light-producing reaction. Light produced by living organisms is called bioluminescence. Fireflies use it to attract mates when they fly at night.

Foxfire

Some types of toadstool emit bioluminescent light at night, perhaps to attract gnats that spread their spores. The light from glowing toadstools is known as foxfire and was used to illuminate one of the world's first submarines.

DYNAMO LIGHT

PUMP THE HANDLE to shine the light. Hand-powered flashlights harness the energy of the human body to generate light, meaning disposable batteries are never needed.

Handle

Squeeze or wind?

Dynamo flashlights can be powered by squeezing a handle or winding a crank. Models vary in the way they store energy, some using a rechargeable battery and others using a flywheel (a spinning wheel).

Squeeze!

Toothed arm

Gear

Wind-up flashlight

Electric flashlight

THIS X-RAY reveals the hidden mechanism inside a hand-powered flashlight. The toothed arm of the handle turns a gear that spins a flywheel. The flywheel keeps the dynamo spinning, while the handle springs back for another squeeze, so the bulb stays lit.

Inside a dynamo

Hand-powered flashlights make use of the dynamo. English scientist Michael Faraday discovered the principle of the dynamo in 1831 when he found that **spinning a magnet** inside a coil of wire created an electric current in the wire. All the electricity **generated** in power plants today is made using this idea.

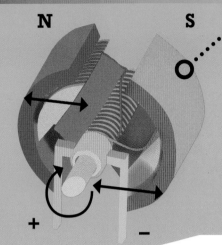

A circular magnet is wrapped around a coil of wire. As the wire spins inside the magnet, electricity starts to flow in the wire.

Incandescent bulb

Reflector

Flywheel and dynamo

Spring

Spare bulb

LARGE FLASHLIGHTS use incandescent bulbs, which contain a tungsten wire that glows when electricity flows through it. Smaller flashlights use LED bulbs.

THERE'S NOTHING COOLER than the minty taste of toothpaste. You use it every day, but exactly what's in the stuff? And also—how do they get the stripes to come out of the tube so evenly? You'll find out here.

Brushing keeps your teeth sparkling.

Plaque under the microscope.

Why do you need to brush?

Your mouth is full of bacteria. They coat your teeth in a thin film called plaque and feed on the things you eat and drink. Bacteria produce acid, which can erode your teeth and cause cavities, and smelly sulfur compounds that cause bad breath.

What's in your toothpaste?

Detergents are soapy substances that foam up and help dislodge food and plaque.

Humectants keep the toothpaste moist and give it its texture.

Flavorings and colorants make it taste nice and look attractive on the brush.

Preservatives stop bacteria from growing in the toothpaste.

Abrasives are made from ground-up rock or chalk. Brushing pushes them against the teeth to remove any stuck-on food and polish away stains.

Thickeners also give the toothpaste texture and stop it from falling off the brush.

There are many different things inside the paste.

Making stripes

Toothpaste isn't put into the tube in **stripes**—they would all get squashed together as they came out. Instead, the tube is mostly filled with a white carrier toothpaste. An outlet pipe leads from the toothpaste to the exit nozzle.

Around this outlet pipe are areas of colored paste. When you squeeze the tube, white toothpaste is forced through the outlet pipe to the nozzle. At the same time, the colored paste is forced through small holes into the outlet pipe, making colored stripes on the white toothpaste.

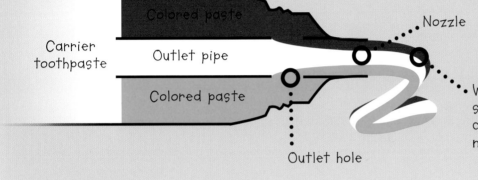

Colored paste

Carrier toothpaste

Outlet pipe

Colored paste

Nozzle

When the tube is squeezed, toothpaste comes out of the nozzle in stripes.

Outlet hole

MINTY FRESHNESS
The cold, tingly feeling you get when you brush your teeth comes from a chemical called menthol, which is found in mint leaves. It triggers special sensors in the mouth and on the tongue that are sensitive to cold. Menthol doesn't actually cool your mouth, it just makes it feel cold.

Fluoride is sometimes added to toothpaste because it helps strengthen your teeth.

SODA FIZZ

UNSCREW A BOTTLE CAP or pull the ring on a can of carbonated soda and whoosh— suddenly the soda rushes to the top to meet you. This mini-eruption is exactly what happens when a volcano spews out magma. It's all because of gas.

Bubbling up

The **fizz** in a bottle of soda comes from **carbon dioxide gas**. This is forced into the drink at high pressure so that it dissolves in the liquid, forming carbonic acid. Once the lid is put on the can or bottle, the gas stays dissolved.

There are millions of bubbles in a glass of soda.

The pressure inside the bottle is twice that of the atmosphere outside.

When the bottle is sitting on a shelf, the pressure is constant, so no bubbles form.

How cool is this?

Soda fountain

If you put a slice of lemon or an ice cube into a carbonated drink, all the bubbles cluster around it. This happens because rough surfaces allow bubbles to attach themselves and grow bigger. If you drop a candy into a carbonated drink, its surface provides places for bubbles to form and, as its sugar dissolves, it forces the carbon dioxide out of the drink. It comes out so fast, the liquid shoots up into the air like a fountain!

As soon as you undo the lid, the pressure is released and bubbles start to form again. They keep expanding as they move toward the surface and pop when they hit the air. Bubbles keep on forming until all of the gas is gone and the drink goes "flat."

So many bubbles arrive at the surface they form a froth.

As the pressure in the neck returns to normal, microbubbles form and expand in the soda.

VOLCANOES ERUPT in the same way as a shaken bottle of soda. Magma contains dissolved gases that stay in the solution as long as it remains underground. During an eruption, this pressure is released. Some magmas contain a lot of gas and explode violently. Others have less gas and pour out gently.

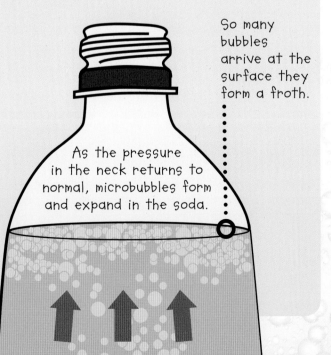

Shaking the bottle creates small whirlpools of low pressure, which allow bubbles to grow quickly.

ELECTRONIC INK

IF PAPER HADN'T BEEN INVENTED, you wouldn't be reading this book. But once it's been printed, paper can't be used again without recycling. Paper is heavy and books take up a lot of space. This is where electronic ink comes in.

Electronic ink looks like regular ink, but if you magnify it you will see the difference.

Plastic paper

Electronic ink is not used for printing, like an ordinary book. Instead, it is sandwiched between two sheets of **flexible plastic**. The ink is made up of millions of tiny capsules, each the width of a human hair, suspended in oil. The bottom layer of plastic is printed with electronic circuits that can be changed to form new patterns of letters.

There are more than 100,000 capsules in every square inch of electronic paper.

Inside the capsules are tiny particles: negatively charged black, and positively charged white. When the circuit pattern changes, the particles move toward areas with the opposite charge.

Black and white particles

This capsule displays as black.

Capsules can show both black and white to make the edges of letters smoother.

– = Negative charge   **+** = Positive charge

The size and *font* of the LETTERING in e-books can be CHANGED to make it *easier* to read.

E-books

Many books are now available electronically as e-books. Digital book readers use **electronic paper** for their display units. When you turn a page, the **circuits** switch the colored particles in the **capsules** to display the correct letters and words for that page. You can **download** a whole book in seconds from the **Internet**.

1%   4584

THOUSANDS of books can be stored on one reader. E-books can also include sound and video to make the book interactive.

ELECTRONIC paper display screens allow devices like e-book readers and cell phones to be light and thin.

This capsule displays as white.

What's next?

The next step is to make a system that can display colored images. Electronic paper could then be used in wallpaper or even clothing. One possibility is to use it for camouflage on military vehicles—one minute your tank is hidden against a wall, the next, it can blend into a desert background, simply by flicking a switch.

Where did that tank come from?

Electronic ink

SOCCER BALL

A CLASSIC SOCCER BALL is based on a shape discovered by the Greek scientist Archimedes more than 2,000 years ago. For decades, this was considered the perfect ball, until scientists realized they could better it. Since then, the search for the ultimate ball has continued.

Perfect geometry

The most familiar-looking soccer ball is made of **12 pentagons** and **20 hexagons** tiled together to form a shape called a truncated icosahedron. This shape, discovered by Archimedes, was first used for the World Cup in 1970. In 2006, it was replaced with the Teamgeist, a ball made of **14 curved panels**. Then the 2010 World Cup used the Jabulani, which has only **8 curved panels**.

Traditional ball

Teamgeist ball

Jabulani ball

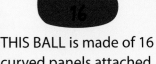

THIS BALL is made of 16 curved panels attached together. Because the seams affect the ball's flight, modern balls are seamless and have fewer sections.

BALLS BOUNCE by storing energy when they're compressed (squashed) and releasing it again when they spring back into shape.

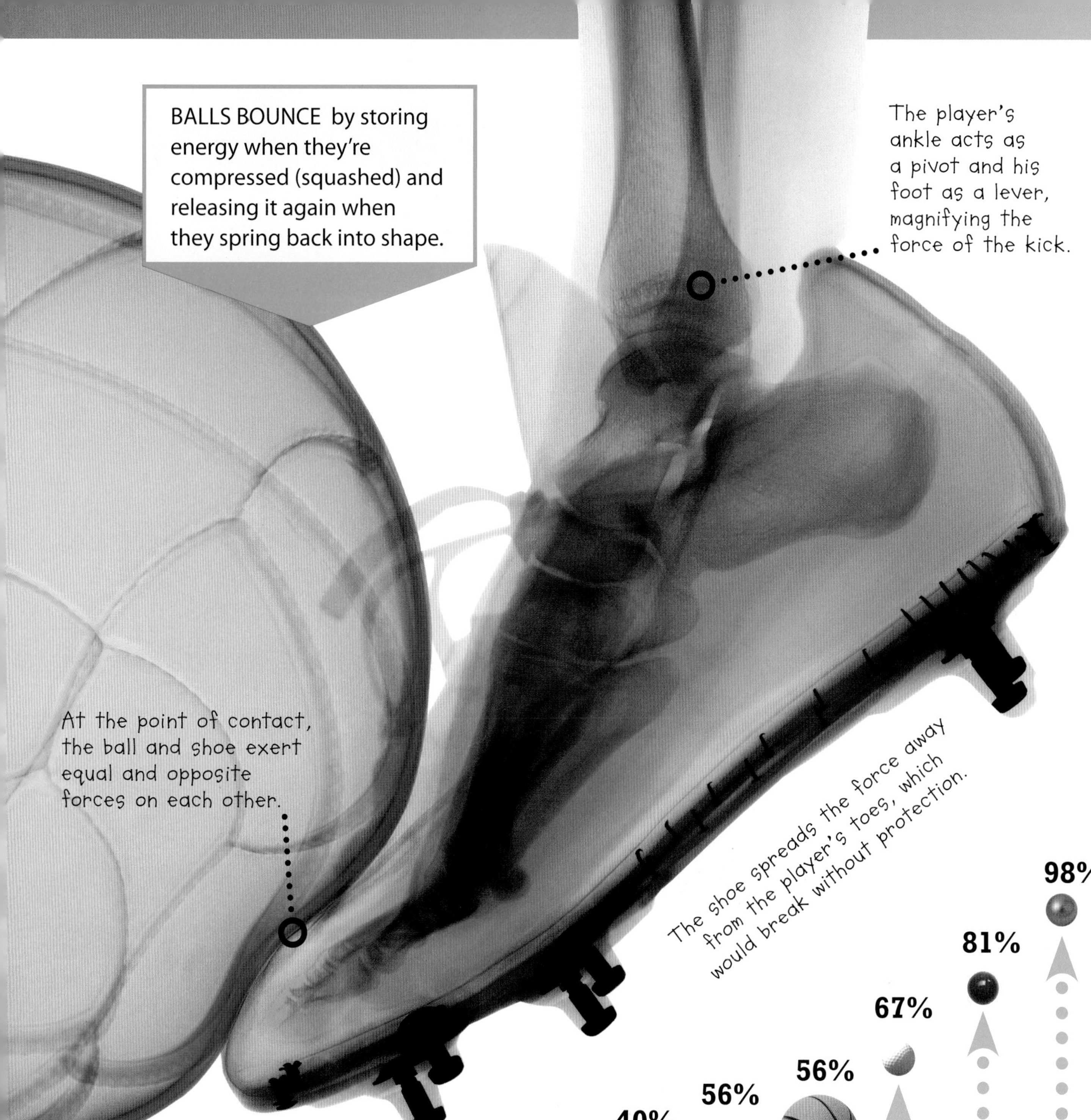

The player's ankle acts as a pivot and his foot as a lever, magnifying the force of the kick.

At the point of contact, the ball and shoe exert equal and opposite forces on each other.

The shoe spreads the force away from the player's toes, which would break without protection.

98%

81%

67%

56%

56%

40%

30%

0%

Soft ball

Soccer ball

Tennis ball

Basketball

Golf ball

Pool ball

Steel ball

Juggling ball

How high?

The height a ball will bounce depends on what it is made of, and how quickly it returns to its shape after it hits the floor. Soft balls spread out and lose energy so they don't bounce back as far as hard balls.

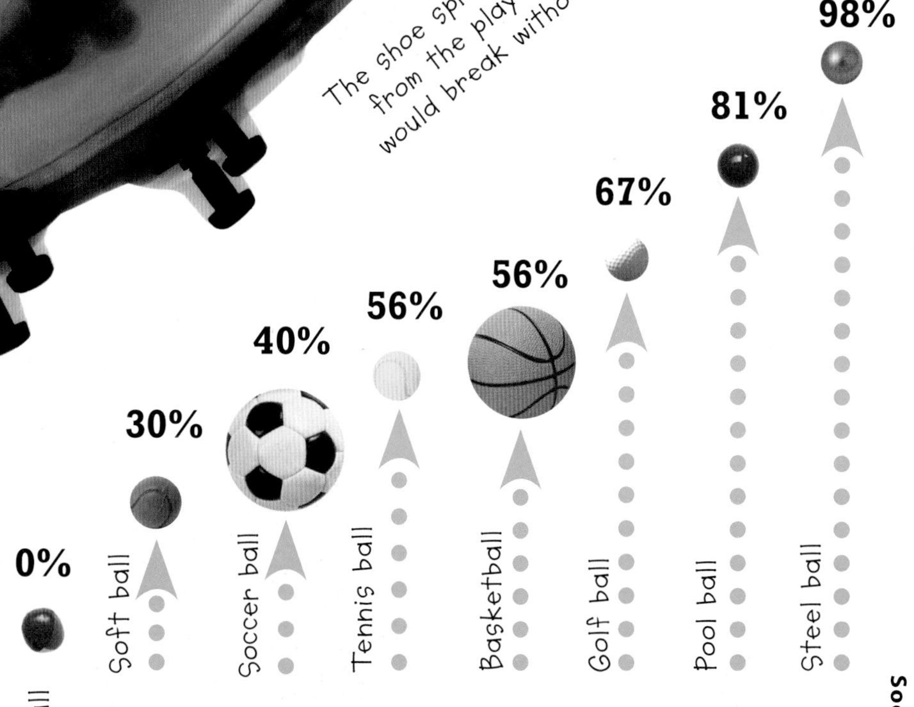

The harder a ball is, the higher it bounces.

BARCODE

EVERY ITEM SOLD in a store bears its own fingerprint: a barcode. A barcode is simply a number converted into a strip of black and white stripes that can be read by a beam of light. But what does the number mean?

840251 000321

Barcodes can be turned into imaginative designs yet still remain readable.

Barcode basics

Most barcodes stand for a 12- or 13-digit number. Different parts of this number identify the company that made the product, the specific product, and often the country of origin. The final digit helps the scanner to double-check that it read all the other digits correctly.

This is the barcode for the US edition of this book.

5 1 5 9 9

US barcodes include an extra section that shows the price ($15.99 here) or other information.

978 0 7566 8604 8

Barcodes for books always start with 978

Geographical area

Publishing company

Product code

Check digit

Reading the code

When a **laser** scans the barcode, light is reflected back from the pattern of lines. A **sensor** inside the scanner times the reflections, which **measures** the widths of the bars. Each digit from 0 to 9 has a particular combination of four bars in alternating black and white. The colors don't matter—only the thickness. The digit zero, for instance, is coded by a thick bar followed by a medium followed by two thin bars. It can be black-white-black-white or white-black-white-black.

The scanner fires a red laser beam at the barcode and picks up the reflected pattern of light at the same time.

BARCODE

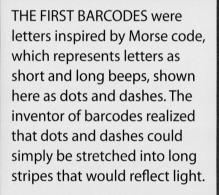

THE FIRST BARCODES were letters inspired by Morse code, which represents letters as short and long beeps, shown here as dots and dashes. The inventor of barcodes realized that dots and dashes could simply be stretched into long stripes that would reflect light.

A 2-D barcode (also called a QR code) can pack more information into a much smaller area.

Next generation

The latest barcodes consist of a grid of black and white or colored patterns that pack in more data. These patterns sometimes contain hidden web links that customers can decode by scanning the image with a cell phone. Both of these barcodes link to the DK website.

High-capacity color barcodes consist of colored triangles.

NEON LIGHTS

SHINING OUT FROM BUILDINGS, neon signs light up the night sky. These glass tubes can be bent to form shapes or spell out words. What makes them different from ordinary light bulbs is that they produce colored, rather than white, light.

NEON LIGHTS get their name from the gas that some of the tubes are filled with. It is this gas that produces the color. Neon is one of a group of elements called the noble gases. The other noble gases are helium, argon, krypton, xenon, and radon. Each glows a specific color when electricity is passed through it.

Handmade

All neon lights are handmade. To make them bend, they have to be heated carefully in exactly the right place, otherwise they crack.

GOLD is made by mixing argon and helium and putting them in a gold glass tube.

REDS and **ORANGES** are produced by passing electricity through neon gas, which is usually colorless.

GREEN is made when argon is put into tubes lined with a green fluorescent coating. Krypton also produces green colors.

AMBER is what you get when neon is used in green fluorescent tubes.

PINK is a combination of argon and xenon gases, or simply argon in a purple fluorescent tube.

BLUE is made by adding a small amount of mercury vapor to argon. Argon on its own glows a faint purple.

WHITE is given out by xenon gas. Alternatively, mercury vapor is used in a fluorescent tube.

BUBBLE GUM

BLOWING A GUM BUBBLE and seeing how big it will go before it goes pop is fun. Even scraping it off your face afterward adds to the pleasure. But have you ever thought about what it is you are chewing? Or what helps you to blow a really big bubble? It's all down to chemistry.

Balls of bubble gum are dipped in candy coating.

A long stretch

The first chewing gum used a tree sap called **chicle**. This comes from the **sapodilla tree.** But one tree can only produce a small amount each year, so synthetic gums are used instead. These soften in the mouth like chicle. Sugar is added to help the gum hold its flavor. Sometimes coloring is added.

The chemical chains in gum are linked together, which helps it to stretch and then go back to its original shape.

Gum's original shape

Gum was first chewed by the ancient Greeks and the Mayans of Central America. They used natural saps and gums that oozed from trees. These weren't sweet, but were very chewy.

Stretched gum

Chicle, like **rubber**, is naturally stretchy. It is made of long-chain chemicals that are usually curled up, but pull out straight when stretched. They go back to their curly state when you stop pulling on them. Gum is basically an edible **rubber band**.

The RECORD for the world's BIGGEST BUBBLE GUM bubble currently stands at 23 in (58 cm), measured from the lips to the far end of the bubble.

BUBBLE GUM has a slightly different formula from chewing gum and can be blown more easily. To blow a really big bubble, first you need to chew the gum for about five minutes. This makes the sugar dissolve out of the gum. Since sugar makes the bubble pop, you need to get rid of it before you can blow a BIG bubble.

BALLOON

YOU HEAR THE BANG, but this is the moment you never see—when a balloon goes pop! It all happens in the blink of an eye and so fast that your brain can't take it in. But with the magic of high-speed photography you can see exactly what's going on.

THIS BALLOON has been filled with flour to show what happens when it bursts. Just a fraction of a second after sticking a pin into it, the rubber cracks and a split tears around it at lightning speed. When a balloon goes pop, the edges of the rubber shrink rapidly, causing a shock wave. This is what makes the noise.

Rubber bands

Rubber

Balloons are made of a **stretchy substance called rubber**. Rubber is made of long chains of chemicals that twist around each other. When air is pumped in, the chains stretch out and stiffen. When they get too stiff, they are likely to burst.

Float or sink?

Around 200 trillion air molecules are crammed inside a single balloon.

Whether your balloon floats or sinks to the ground depends on what it is filled with. If you blow it up with a **pump**, you push molecules of air into it. The balloon will (sort of) float because it is filled with the same **air** that surrounds it.

Helium is the best gas for inflating a balloon, because it is lighter than air. The only problem is, your balloon will escape very quickly if you let it go!

POP!

If you stick a pin in near the knot, the balloon will not go bang because there is still some stretch left in this part of the balloon.

When you blow a balloon up yourself, your breath includes **carbon dioxide gas**, which is one of the gases you breathe out. This is slightly heavier than air so the balloon will sink.

LIGHTNING

A SUDDEN FLASH OF LIGHTNING is one of the most dramatic events on our planet. Stretching from sky to earth, a brilliant bolt of electricity shoots from a cloud. It does this at an amazing speed of 60,000 miles (100,000 km) a second.

IT ISN'T ONLY LIGHT that is given off when lightning strikes: a huge amount of heat is also produced. The heat given off by the stroke makes the air around it expand rapidly. This expansion causes a shock wave that turns into sound. We hear this as thunder seconds after we see the flash.

The temperature of a lightning bolt can reach 36,000°F (20,000°C)—more than three times hotter than the surface of the Sun.

How does it happen?

No one is exactly sure how lightning forms, but it happens when an **electric charge** builds up in a storm cloud. Raindrops are constantly being swept up and down by air currents. As they collide, they become electrically charged—some molecules become **positive** and others become **negative**. Positive charges build up in the top of the cloud and negative charges collect at the bottom. At the same time, the ground becomes positively charged.

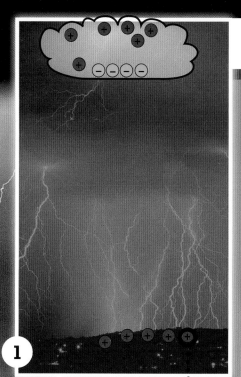

1

There is a very strong attraction between positive and negative charges, so they will always try to join up. An intense electric field starts to build up that will strip electrons from the air molecules, making it easier for electricity to pass through the air.

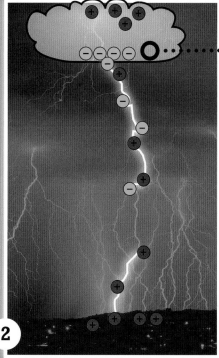

2

When the electric field is strong enough, a pathway starts to form between the cloud and the ground. This first stroke is called a stepped leader. It looks jagged because at this stage there are many possible paths through the air.

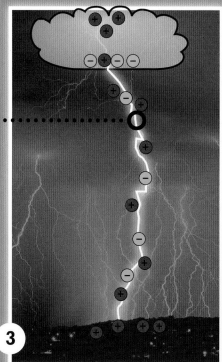

3

As the leader gets closer to the ground, charged particles start to stream upward. When the leader meets a stream, current flows between the cloud and the ground. The current is so strong it makes the air molecules along the path of the strike give off light. Not all lightning hits the ground—many flashes occur between and within clouds.

ROCKET CAR

WHAT DO YOU GET when you put a jet engine from a fighter plane, a Formula 1 car engine, and a rocket together? The fastest car in the world—at least, that's what its makers hope.

Record holder

Ever since the first cars were built, drivers have wanted to go faster. The current land-speed record stands at 763 mph (1,228 kph). It was achieved by Thrust SSC, which used two jet-fighter engines to help it reach supersonic speed. To go beyond this requires more thrust than a jet can provide.

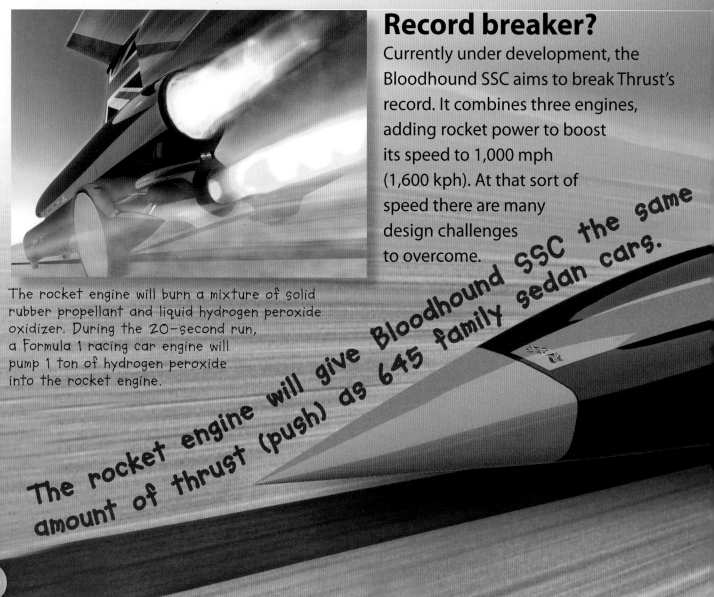

Record breaker?

Currently under development, the Bloodhound SSC aims to break Thrust's record. It combines three engines, adding rocket power to boost its speed to 1,000 mph (1,600 kph). At that sort of speed there are many design challenges to overcome.

The rocket engine will burn a mixture of solid rubber propellant and liquid hydrogen peroxide oxidizer. During the 20-second run, a Formula 1 racing car engine will pump 1 ton of hydrogen peroxide into the rocket engine.

The rocket engine will give Bloodhound SSC the same amount of thrust (push) as 645 family sedan cars.

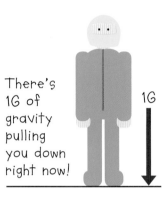

Feeling the force

It's not easy to drive a supersonic car. When it accelerates and decelerates, the driver feels enormous pressures called **G-forces** (the effect of gravity pulling on an object). Everything on Earth feels a pull of **1G**, but forces can reach **3G** in a car slowing down from supersonic speed. Drivers are usually ex-pilots who are trained to cope with the effects of G-forces, which include blurred vision, loss of balance, headaches, and reduced heartbeat.

There's 1G of gravity pulling you down right now!

1G

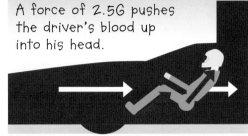

A force of 2.5G pushes the driver's blood up into his head.

Acceleration

A pull of 3G draws the blood into his legs.

Deceleration

The intake draws air into the jet engine.

Jet engine

A Eurofighter engine is being used to provide Bloodhound with extra thrust. When combined with the thrust from the rocket engine, the car will be able to travel 5 miles (8 km) from a standing start in less than 100 seconds.

At high speeds the car will try to take off. To avoid this, it sits as low to the ground as possible. The car is also extremely strong and rigid to cope with air pressure that feels like 40 elephants sitting on it!

STONEPROOF WHEELS
Made of titanium metal, the wheels can withstand stones hitting them at high speed. They have no tires, since no tires exist that can survive 10,000 revolutions (turns) a minute.

Rocket car

CRASH HELMET

PROTECTIVE HEADGEAR can mean the difference between life and death. A crash helmet provides the first line of defense against a violent impact, absorbing the energy of a collision so that your skull and brain don't have to.

A thumbtack concentrates a force into a small area.

Protecting your skull

A plastic mouthguard prevents injuries to the teeth.

A helmet works by **distributing a force** to weaken its effect. A force that's concentrated in a small area causes enormous pressure—think of the way a thumbtack concentrates the force of a finger to create enough pressure to pierce a wall. A helmet does the opposite job, spreading out a force across a wide area to **reduce the pressure**. Some helmets are also designed to break on impact to dissipate the energy further.

A helmet spreads a force across a wide area.

The force of an impact spreads around the whole helmet, resulting in weak pressure on the wearer's head.

Shock-absorbing pads cushion the inside of the helmet.

The human skull acts as a natural, inner crash helmet, providing another layer of protection for the brain.

The cage in a sports helmet protects the jaw and teeth from fast-moving balls.

Although a HELMET reduces the risk of head injury, the neck is unprotected and spinal injuries remain a serious risk.

3-D FILMS

WATCHING A 3-D FILM can make you feel like you're right in the middle of the action, surrounded by the events that are happening on screen rather than viewing them from afar. To create this amazing optical illusion, the movie presents a different image to each eye and so tricks your brain into seeing in 3-D.

Seeing in three dimensions

Our two eyes are set **slightly apart** so that each eye sees a slightly different view. The closer an object is, the more different it looks to the right and left eyes. The brain uses this difference to work out how far away the object is. This ability to judge distance allows us to see in three dimensions.

What we see

Left eye view

Right eye view

Both views are merged in the brain to form a single 3-D image.

How cool is this?

ANAGLYPH LENSES
The simplest 3-D movies are watched through anaglyph glasses, which have red and blue (or green) lenses. The film is a double image made up of overlapping red and blue images filmed by different cameras. When you wear the glasses, each eye sees only one of the overlapping images.

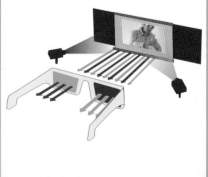

Polarized lenses

Light travels in waves that can wobble up and down or left and right. Polarized lenses block waves that wobble in certain directions, while letting other waves through. As a result, polarized glasses can do just the same job as anaglyph glasses, but without distorting the natural colors of the film.

Active lenses

Active 3-D glasses contain a **liquid crystal layer** that turns black when switched on, blocking light. The image on screen flicks rapidly between two alternative views at the same time as the left and right lenses in the glasses turn black. This system is often used in 3-D televisions.

LIQUID LAMP

THE LIQUID LAMP IS STILL AS COOL TODAY as when it first appeared in the 1960s. Watching the changing shapes of the colored wax as it rises and falls is endlessly fascinating. But did you know that this type of movement is happening right under your feet?

THE SECRET of a liquid lamp relies on the way that the two fluids inside it never mix. Think about oil and water—oil floats on the surface of water. If you shake them up, the oil forms into droplets but never dissolves in the water.

UP AND DOWN
The two liquids used in the lamp are chosen so that one of them will rise and fall when the lamp is switched on. This is a waxy substance that becomes more liquid when it is heated. As the wax warms up, it forms blobs that break away and float to the top of the lamp, which is cooler. When the blobs cool, they sink back to the bottom.

Inside the base is an ordinary light bulb. This heats up the wax and shines through the liquid.

Electricity is needed to power the lamp.

Turning up the heat

Cool wax molecules are tightly packed together and take up a small amount of space.

Cool wax

Warm wax

There is more space between warm wax molecules, which makes the wax less dense.

So why does **heating the wax** make it **float**? The answer lies in how tightly the molecules of wax are packed together. We call this its **density**, which is a measure of how much **mass** is crammed into a particular sized **space**. For example, a cube of soap is less dense than the same-sized cube of heavy lead atoms. The soap would **float** in a bath of water, while the lead would **sink**.

In a liquid lamp, the two fluids have different densities. When the wax is heated its molecules gain **energy** and start **moving** around. They spread out and take up more space. The wax becomes less dense than the other liquid, so it floats. When it cools, the wax molecules pack together more tightly, which increases its density and makes it sink.

Earth as a liquid lamp

Below Earth's surface, a similar process is recycling rocks. Heat from the core melts areas of the rocky mantle, which rise to the surface in plumes. Volcanoes form and erupt the rock onto the surface. At the same time, parts of the crust are being pulled into the mantle and sink because they are cold and dense.

Crust

Outer mantle

Mantle

Core

Cooler, denser rock sinks down into the mantle.

Hot, liquid rock rises to the surface.

Liquid lamp

GALILEO THERMOMETER

Galileo invented this 400 years ago.

SUSPENDED IN A CLEAR GLASS

column, tiny glass globes of colored liquid move up and down. This unusual object is a thermometer. It works because the liquid around the globes changes slightly when the temperature changes, making the globes rise and fall.

As the **temperature** of the air around the thermometer changes, so does the temperature of the oil. As the oil gets warmer, its molecules move **farther apart** and it becomes less dense. When the oil cools, they move closer together and it becomes denser.

THE GLASS COLUMN contains a clear liquid, usually oil. In it are several globes, each with a temperature tag on the bottom. Every globe has a different density (the density of something depends on how much mass is packed into a space). This density hardly changes. But it does make each globe sink at the temperature written on the tag.

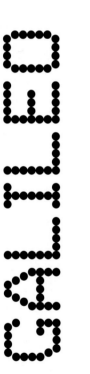

STAYING AFLOAT

Galileo thermometers rely on buoyancy. Buoyancy is the ability of an object to float in a liquid. When you put an object into a liquid it pushes some of the liquid aside. This "displaced" liquid pushes back against the object. If the density of the object is the same or less than the force of the liquid pushing upward, it will float. If it is greater, it will sink.

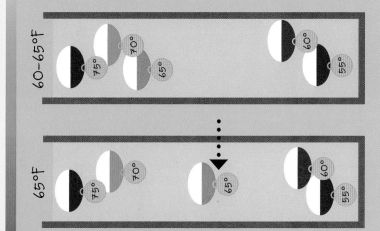

Less dense beach ball floats

Dense golf ball sinks

Measuring temperature

Because each globe has a different density, it will float until the density of the oil is too low to provide enough force to push back against it. The globe will then **sink** to the bottom. When the oil cools and becomes denser, the globe will rise again.

There is usually a gap between the top group of bulbs and the lower group. You tell the temperature of the room from the globe that is still floating in the gap. If there is no globe in the gap, then you know that the temperature is somewhere between that of the two globes on each side of the gap.

...As the oil heats up, it becomes less dense. It reaches the temperature shown on a floating globe—that globe is now more dense than the surrounding oil, so it starts to sink.

75° 70° 65° 60° 55°

60-65°F

65°F

75° 70° 65° 60° 55°

84° 80°

37

SKY LANTERN

PAPER BALLOONS FLOAT INTO THE NIGHT
and soon become distant pinpricks of
light. Used in celebrations all over
Asia, sky lanterns work on
a very simple idea—the
fact that hot air rises.

A heated lantern floats in cool air.

TRADITIONAL SKY LANTERNS are made from
oiled rice paper on a bamboo frame. A small
candle or waxy fuel source heats the air inside
the lantern, making it rise into the air.

THE CHINESE SKY LANTERN FESTIVAL in Taipei marks the end of the Chinese New Year celebrations, with people sending wishes to heaven for good luck. Releasing lanterns started hundreds of years ago, when villages were often under attack. Watchmen released lanterns to show people when it was safe to come home.

When air is heated, the molecules of gas move around more quickly and spread out, so the spaces between the molecules get bigger. As the air **expands** inside the lantern, some of the molecules get pushed out.

Sky lanterns have been mistaken for UFO sightings!

Floating in the air

Hot air balloons work in the same way as sky lanterns—although they have to be much bigger than sky lanterns to lift the weight of the basket, people, and gas burners. The burners are turned on to heat air caught inside the balloon, which makes the balloon rise. Turn the burners off, and gravity pulls the balloon back down toward the ground.

The expanded warm air inside the lantern is now lighter than the surrounding cooler air, so the lantern rises.

WARNING:
A lit sky lantern can burn you. NEVER light or hold a sky lantern without adult supervision.

Sky lantern

CRYSTALS

CRYSTALS ARE EVERYWHERE—sugar, salt, and ice are just a few that you probably see most days. If you look at them closely you will see that they all look very similar. Most crystals form regular shapes and have flat sides.

CRYSTALS CAN FORM when a liquid turns into a solid. If it cools or evaporates slowly at a regular pressure, all the atoms (small particles it is made from) line up in a pattern. The pattern they make depends on what type of atom they are. The smallest number of atoms needed to form the basic shape of the crystal is called a unit cell.

The metal bismuth only forms crystals like these when it is grown in a laboratory.

The shape and symmetry of a crystal depends on how its atoms are arranged. This is called its **system**. There are seven systems, but some crystals can form **mixtures** of more than one system.

The structure and color of the crystal affects the way it reflects light. Diamonds are cut and polished to reflect as much light as possible. ....O

How big?

Crystal size varies from microscopic to the enormous 33 ft (10 m) selenite crystals found in a cave in Mexico. Selenite is named after the Greek for "Moon" because of its white reflections.

Many living organisms can make crystals— snails use them to make their shells. ....O

Crystal systems

Cubic	Tetragonal	Orthorhombic	Triclinic	Monoclinic	Hexagonal	Trigonal

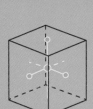

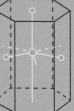

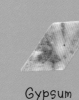

Iron pyrite	Zircon	Sulfur	Microcline	Gypsum	Aquamarine	Sapphire

BIOMETRICS

EVERY HUMAN BODY IS UNIQUE.

Even identical twins are slightly different. Some of these differences are so specific, they can be used to pick one person out of millions of others. This makes them ideal for security devices. The main systems use fingerprints and eye scans.

WHAT ARE BIOMETRICS?
This is a way of identifying people by comparing detailed measurements of parts of their body, such as the distance between the eyes. Biometrics can also identify someone by the sound of his voice or his handwriting.

Fingerprints

Look at your fingertips. Each finger has a pattern of swirls and ridges that is different from everyone else's. When a finger is first placed on a scanner, the scanner picks up the **patterns** and records them in a database. When the finger is scanned again, the computer searches the database, looking for features, such as the end of a ridge, and tries to find a pattern that matches.

The scanner joins features to make a pattern of straight lines. When it matches these lines on two sets of prints, it can identify a person.

#10019123-050

Although fingerprints are unique, they do change over time because of cuts, burns, or even loss of a finger. It is also relatively easy to copy someone's fingerprint to steal their identity. You could even be mistaken for a koala—they have very similar fingerprints to humans.

Iris scanning

First, a person looks into an iris scanner.

A camera takes a picture of the eye.

A computer locates each tiny feature...

...and turns it into code.

Eyeballs are another part of the body that can be identified. One method uses the iris, the colored ring of muscles at the front of your eye. The color and patterns of the muscles are unique, and can be plotted like the coordinates on a map and stored on a computer. The eyes are scanned using ordinary and infrared light (which picks up the features of dark-colored eyes). Iris scans are **10 times** more accurate than fingerprints.

FLYING DISK

A FLYING DISK, more often known as a frisbee, is great for a game in the park on a sunny day. The disk was invented in the United States around the mid 1940s. A modern disk is made from plastic and has a slightly curved top surface, which helps it to fly.

Up, up, and away...

Spin gives the disk stability and keeps it moving forward.

Angle of attack—launching the disk at a slight angle to the ground helps minimize the effects of drag.

THE IMPORTANCE OF SPIN
Throwing the disk in the air provides lift, but unless you spin it at the same time it will quickly fall to the ground. Spinning gives the disk extra stability as it flies. The faster it spins, the more stable it is.

Flying ring

Flying rings can go much farther than disks and are better flyers. At only ¼ in (3 mm) thick they slice through

The hole helps it fly!

the air because they produce less drag. They have a spoiler (a slightly raised edge) on the rim that helps keep the lift at the center of the ring.

As air passes over the upper surface of the disk it speeds up. This creates an area of low pressure at the top of the disk. At the same time, the air below the disk slows down and creates an area of high pressure. This difference in pressure is what lifts the disk in the air.

Weight

The curved rim pushes the air over the top of the disk. A disk without a rim is less stable in flight.

AIR

Drag

Drag is a force that pushes against the disk as it's flying and slows it down.

Thrust

Lift

Lift is an upward force that counteracts the weight of the disk and keeps it in the air.

Boomerang

A boomerang moves through the air in the same way as a flying disk. Its upper surface is **curved** like an airplane wing so that air speeds up as it passes over the top and creates lift. If you throw it horizontally it will lift up and fly in a straight line. But if you want your boomerang **to come back**, then you should hold it at one end and throw it almost vertically so that it **turns end over end**. A good flick of the wrist makes the boomerang fly on a curved path and brings it back to you.

Spin makes the top part of the wing move through the air faster than the bottom part, which gives the boomerang more lift.

JET PACK

PEOPLE HAVE LONG DREAMED OF FLYING like birds, but no one has come closer than daredevil Swiss inventor Yves Rossy. The only man in history to have swooped though the skies with a jet-powered wing pack, Rossy has made more than 30 flights with his invention, including a nine-minute trip across the English Channel from France to England.

In 2010, Rossy leaped from this balloon over Switzerland to perform two aerial loops.

Into the blue

After being lifted by a balloon or plane, Rossy ignites the engines of his jet pack and leaps into the blue. The fuel lasts up to 20 minutes, and a parachute is released for landing. Enormous care is needed to keep the wing stable in flight and prevent an uncontrollable spin.

Early versions of the wing were hinged to allow Rossy to jump out of plane doors, but these were too unstable to fly safely.

The flight begins with a steep, headfirst dive. The pilot then maneuvers his body into a horizontal position to fly forward or climb.

The wings are made of carbon fiber—a kind of plastic reinforced by microscopic strands of carbon. This material is amazingly strong yet lightweight.

With a jet pack you really can fly like a bird!

On the wing

The **carbon fiber** wing pack is 6½ ft (2 m) wide and has four **jet engines** similar to the engines found on model jet aircraft. Power is controlled with a small hand-operated **throttle**. To steer, climb, or dive, the pilot simply adjusts the position of his body.

Visor protects the face from fierce winds.

Altimeter shows height above the ground.

Harness

Kerosene-burning engines

Hand throttle

Heat-resistant suit protects body from hot jet exhaust.

Hey, look at him! Just who does he think he is???

RAINBOW

JUST AFTER A SHOWER OF RAIN, YOU MAY SEE A RAINBOW. It arrives out of nowhere and vanishes just as quickly. You can never reach the end of a rainbow, since it always remains the same distance away. That's because it's a trick of the light.

RAINBOWS APPEAR when the atmosphere is full of water droplets. This can be during a rainstorm, when it's foggy, or near a waterfall. You will always find a rainbow on the opposite side of the sky to the Sun.

Light colors

Sunlight is made up of different wavelengths of light. Each wavelength has a color, but when they are all mixed together they look white. You can see that a ray of light has different colors because it bends as it passes through a glass prism. Each wavelength bends at a slightly different angle, with blue bending more than red, so the colors separate out into a band of colors including red, yellow, green, blue, and violet. These are the colors you see in a rainbow.

When sunlight hits a water droplet, it bends and reflects to make a band of colors.

Rainbows appear only when the Sun is low in the sky and you are standing with your back to it.

Seeing a rainbow

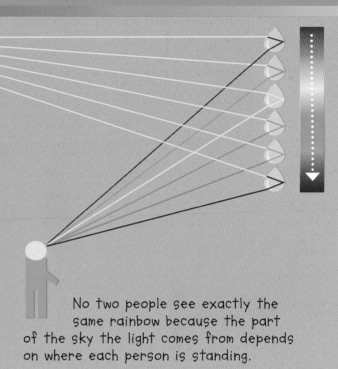

Just like in a prism, a ray of sunlight bends and reflects off the **curved surfaces** of a water droplet before emerging again as a band of colors. As each drop falls, it briefly flashes its colors before another droplet replaces it. You see **only one color**, depending on the height of the droplet and the angle the light makes with your eyes.

No two people see exactly the same rainbow because the part of the sky the light comes from depends on where each person is standing.

Double rainbows

Sometimes another rainbow appears outside the main bow. These occur when light is reflected twice before leaving the droplet. This reverses the sequence of colors seen in the second bow.

Rainbows always appear as an arc in the sky. In fact, rainbows always form a circle, but part of it lies below the horizon. The lower the Sun is in the sky, the more of the circle you will see. If you're up in an airplane, you may even see the full circle.

NIGHT VISION

HUMANS ARE NOT GOOD AT SEEING THINGS IN THE DARK. No matter how many carrots you eat, you will never be able to sneak up on a cat at night. Our eyes are built for looking at things in daylight. If you want to see what a cat sees in the dark, you have to use night vision goggles—a set of electronic eyes that increase the amount of light.

Many animals that hunt at night have a mirrorlike structure at the back of their eyes that reflects light back into the eyes so they can see better. This is why their eyes shine when you point a flashlight at them.

Night vision goggles

Our eyes do their best to capture as many particles of light (called **photons**) as possible. We only see things because **light** bounces off them, so when it's dark, there are fewer photons to pick up. Night vision goggles work by turning photons into **electrons** (tiny particles that have an electrical charge). The number of electrons can easily be increased and turned back into more photons.

1 Photons of light enter through a **lens**. All the colors are there, but it is difficult to detect them at night.

2 The **photocathode** converts the photons into electrons.

3 A **photomultiplier** increases the number of electrons.

4 The electrons then hit a **phosphor screen** and give off tiny flashes of light.

5 Now that there are more photons than entered the lens, the **image** appears much brighter.

Light

Image

Now you see it...

WHY GREEN? The image you see is formed when the electrons hit a phosphor screen. A zinc sulfide phosphor is chosen to give off photons of a green color because it is a comfortable color to look at for long periods. The image shows up as areas of light and dark green, depending on how many electrons hit that part of the screen.

Phosphors are chemicals that give off light when they are hit by electrons. This type of light is called luminescence.

Night vision goggles help you see objects even when it is completely dark.

LOCKS

EVERYONE HAS SOMETHING THEY THINK IS PRECIOUS or that they don't want others to see or get into. So how do you keep it safe? The answer is to use a lock. Locks are ancient mechanisms, first invented by the Egyptians 4,000 years ago.

Lots of locks

Locks vary from simple ratchets that push a bolt into a hole to complicated mixtures of pins and wheels that can create an infinite number of combinations. The lock on your front door is probably a cylinder lock, which uses two sets of pins of different lengths.

The right key will push the pins up so the two sets meet evenly.

The top set of pins is pushed above the cylinder, allowing it to turn and the lock to open.

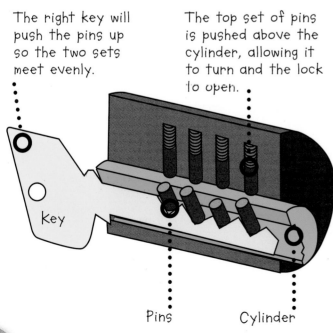

Key

Pins Cylinder

Cylinder padlock

Just like a cylinder lock, a cylinder padlock has two sets of pins. Above each set is a spring that holds the pins in place. When you put the key in the lock, the jagged edge pushes the pins upward. When the top set of pins is clear of the cylinder (which can only be done with the right key), the shackle is released.

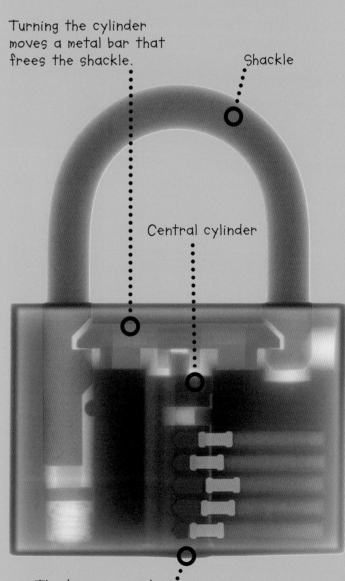

Turning the cylinder moves a metal bar that frees the shackle.

Shackle

Central cylinder

The key goes in here

Lever lock

Also known as mortice locks, lever locks use a key to lift levers and release a lock. There can be between two and seven levers inside a lever lock. A lever only moves if it matches with the right key bit, and there are usually seven variations of bit shapes for each lever.

A seven−lever lock has 7×7×7×7×7×7×7 variations—that's 823,543 different key combinations!

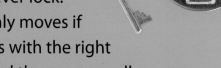

Levers •••••

The key turns here...

2

3

1

... and the bolt slides across to release the shackle.

... the levers lift up...

Combination lock

This lock is made up of a series of wheels, each with a protruding part called a tooth on the front and back. As you turn the dial to the first number of the combination, the first wheel turns and the tooth on its back connects with the tooth on the front of the next wheel. This process continues every time a number is dialed until all the wheels move together. When they are all connected, a notch at the top of each wheel lines up and allows a piece of metal called the fence to drop into it. This lifts the bar holding the shackle closed.

Metal bar lifts when the combination is correct.

When the notches are lined up the fence drops into the gap.

Numbered wheels

ROBOT DOG

WANT A DOG that never needs to go outside or visit the vet? Then maybe a robot dog is the pet for you. These friendly robots are programmed to behave just like a real animal. Your mechanical pet will also respond to commands, recognize faces and toys, and remember favorite places.

The dog wags its tail when it's happy.

Artificial intelligence

All robots think and react using artificial intelligence. This is a computer program that allows a machine to operate on a basic level and learn from experience like a living thing. This robot can learn about where it lives and what its owner likes it to do. It understands more than 100 voice commands and can be programmed to respond in different ways.

Showing emotion

One of the key challenges for robot builders is to get the robot to **show emotion**. Like a real dog, this one makes sounds, wags its tail, plays, and responds to praise or scolding. It also has a set of colored lights on its back that indicate its **mood** or that it is performing a task.

SOUND SENSORS
The dog has microphones for ears that pick up sounds and commands such as "Lie down," or "Sit!" Once it has learned its name, it will come when called. But like a real dog, these robots will not respond if they are feeling unhappy or are not in the mood to play.

DISTANCE SENSORS help the robot detect when it is getting too close to objects, or the edges of a table or step.

SIGHT SENSORS
A camera at the front of its head is programmed to look for faces. When the dog sees someone it recognizes, a pattern of lights is displayed on its face. It will flash a different pattern or bark when it sees a favorite toy.

Tiny motors make the head and limbs move.

Many sensors work together.

MOTION SENSORS detect movement when you wave toys in front of them and the dog will follow the movement with its head. The sensors also help the robot balance while moving.

Inside you can see many microchips, wires, and circuit boards.

TOUCH SENSORS on the chin, head, and back respond to stroking or patting the dog. It also has a sensor on each paw so it can touch objects.

Pressure sensor

FRACTALS

HAVE YOU EVER LOOKED AT A FERN LEAF, or the frost on a windowpane? What you will see is a pattern that, when you look even closer, repeats itself. Patterns like these are called fractals.

Frost is a branching fractal.

Take a close look at this Romanesco broccoli—each of its conical florets is a copy of the larger vegetable.

Natural fractals

Nature is full of fractals. The most common are branching and spiral fractals. Branching fractals include blood vessels, tree branches, river networks, lightning, and brain cells. Spirals range from galaxies and hurricane clouds to the growth pattern of an ammonite shell, or the curled-up fronds of a fern.

FRACTALS ARE EVERYWHERE. They are never-ending patterns that repeat themselves at different scales—from large to small and from small to large. Zoom in on any part of a fractal and you will see that it looks very like a larger piece. But not quite—there will be some tiny differences. Once nature finds an easy way to do something, it tries to repeat the pattern.

The lines between the chambers of this ammonite show a fractal pattern that is repeated every time a new chamber is added to the shell.

MATHEMATICAL FRACTALS

Mathematical equations can be turned into beautiful fractals with the help of a computer. Because even simple equations produce complex fractals, mathematicians can use data from random events like the weather to draw a fractal and find an equation to predict future weather patterns.

Fractals are increasingly being used in science and engineering. For example:

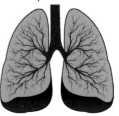

Medicine uses fractals to help design structures that can be used to grow replacement blood vessels and other body tissues, such as lungs.

Cell phones now use fractal antennas because they fit inside the phone and can pick up many frequencies.

Computer models use fractals to work out how coral reefs will grow and to help predict future weather patterns.

Fractals are everywhere you look.

Most fractals look very complex, but they are easy to make. You just keep repeating the process over and over again. A geometric fractal called the Sierpinski Triangle is made by removing a central triangle from the ones that have just been created.

Fractals

FIREWORKS

STREAKING ACROSS THE SKY and exploding into bursts of bright color, fireworks light up the night sky. Fireworks are tubes of powdered chemicals that ignite when a fuse is lit.

Inside a shell

The chemicals are packed into cardboard tubes, or **shells**. The center of the shell is packed with gunpowder and a fuse. Surrounding the core is more gunpowder and pellets called **stars**, which produce the color. There may also be small particles of metal, such as magnesium or zinc, to provide sparkly effects.

To get GREEN fireworks, add barium.

At large displays the shells are launched from steel pipes. A lifting charge blasts the shell into the air and ignites the fuse.

BLUE is hard to produce—but copper chloride works well.

Lighting the fuse ignites the bursting charge and makes the shell explode at the right height.

Bursting charge

Gunpowder

Stars

For ORANGE fireworks, calcium and carbon give the best color.

To get RED colors lithium or strontium is added.

YELLOW colors are made by adding sodium.

Early fireworks were mainly orange, yellow, or white. Modern fireworks use different metal compounds to produce a wide range of colors.

Sky patterns

The patterns fireworks make depend on how the **stars** are packed into the shell. There are often several fuses that ignite different parts of the firework at different times to help create the effect.

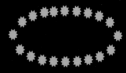

Ring: this forms a bright circle of stars.

Willow: stars fall in trails from a central point to the ground.

Fish: a swarm of tiny stars that streak in all directions across the sky.

Serpentine: groups of stars zigzag as they fall.

Chrysanthemum: lots of small trailing stars that look like the flower.

SNOW

The simplest and smallest type of snow crystal is a HEXAGONAL PRISM. This six-sided shape forms a basic snowflake—a plate.

SNOW IS SIMPLY WATER that has frozen solid. Water exists in the atmosphere as a gas, or vapor. When there is a lot of vapor it forms clouds, and then falls as rain. But if the temperature in the cloud is below freezing point, it turns into ice crystals and falls as snow.

The perfect snowball

Ever wondered why some snow is useless for making snowballs? It's because it's **too dry** and **powdery** and won't stick together. This happens if the temperature is **well below freezing point** when it falls. Try holding it in your hands for a while so that it starts to melt, or find some that has been near a house or other warm object. Digging down to a deeper layer also helps—early snow has already melted a bit and been squashed.

Slightly wet snow is best for snowballs!

SNOWFLAKES start out as simple flat shapes called plates. As they get bigger, branches start to develop at the corners. These branches grow in so many different ways, it's likely that no two snowflakes are ever the same.

When a snowflake has six broad arms like a star, it's called a STELLAR PLATE. Each arm has identical markings.

Some snowflakes look like tiny columns. When they get blown around in a cloud, plates start to form at one or both ends. Then they are called CAPPED COLUMNS.

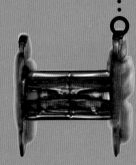

The largest snow crystals are FERN-LIKE STELLAR DENDRITES. These are more than 1/4 in (5 mm) across.

BULLETS are columns that grow to a point at one end. Sometimes a plate grows at the other. Bullet clusters occur when a number of crystals form from the same grain of ice.

STELLAR DENDRITES are usually about 1/4 in (2–4 mm) across and can easily be seen. These make the best powder snow for skiing.

Crystal shapes

Snow crystals are very complex and there may be as many as 40 main types. All are hexagonal (six-sided) in shape because of the way that water molecules line up when they form a solid.

NEEDLES only form when the temperature dips to 23°F (−5°C).

THERMAL IMAGING

THERMAL IMAGING IS USED TO DETECT OBJECTS you can't see when it is dark, smoky, or foggy. It works by measuring the amount of heat something is giving off. A special type of camera is used to take pictures, but instead of using visible light, it uses infrared light. We can't see infrared—we just feel it as heat—but the camera can see it.

HOT

Uses

Thermal imaging can be used for many different purposes:

Doctors look for tumors and other medical problems inside the body before they operate.

Firefighters use infrared cameras to search for people trapped in smoky buildings.

Military personnel use it for surveillance and during nighttime operations.

Sailors use infrared to help them navigate safely at night.

Search and rescue teams use it to locate people lost at sea or stuck on mountains.

Energy conservation specialists use it to see where energy is leaking out of buildings.

Infrared camera

A sensor in the camera detects **infrared light** and turns the readings into **visible colors**. Cool objects show up as purples and blues, and hot objects as yellows and reds. The hottest areas are shown in white.

Thermal imaging is often used to check buildings and machinery for defects that can't be seen.

This thermal imaging camera looks like an ordinary camcorder.

Cold

Hot

The temperature of your skin shows up as reds and yellows. Your hair is cooler, so it looks green.

ALL OBJECTS give off infrared light according to their temperature. When viewed through a thermal imaging camera, hot objects stand out against a cool background and cool objects against a warm background. So you can use it to see things that might not be visible to the naked eye.

An ice pop shows up as black on a thermal imaging picture—so do a cold mouth and fingers!

RADIO

TURN ON A RADIO and out of nowhere, sounds blare out. They have been around you all the time, but you couldn't hear them. That's because they travel through space as energy waves, like light. To receive and hear them you need a radio.

Radio waves travel at the speed of light: 186,000 miles per second.

Inside a radio

The main parts of a radio are the detector, the antenna, the tuner, the amplifier, and the loudspeaker.

Antenna—this picks up all radio signals.

Tuner—this separates out the radio wave you want from the millions of others being transmitted.

Loudspeaker—this takes the electrical signals from the tuner and amplifier and turns them into sound waves.

Amplifier—this boosts the signal and increases the power to the loudspeakers.

Detector—this decodes the radio wave and turns it into an electrical signal that can be turned back into sound.

SIGNALS ARE SENT OUT by antennae from radio or TV stations. These encode information about the sound or picture so that it can be carried by a radio wave.

Energy waves

Radio and visible light are both a type of energy wave called electromagnetic radiation. Radio waves have longer wavelengths than visible light waves.

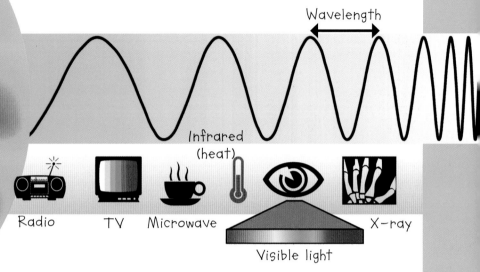

Wavelength

Infrared (heat)

Radio   TV   Microwave   X-ray

Visible light

We can only see certain wavelengths of energy.

Sound waves

Radio waves and sound waves are not the same. Sound waves are actually **waves of pressure** caused by vibrating objects pushing air molecules together and apart. When they arrive at your ear they make your eardrum vibrate. The vibrations make tiny hairs in your inner ear move, and these movements are turned into nerve signals and sent to the brain.

DIGITAL RADIO CODE Radio stations send out radio waves that include a code of 1s and 0s. The waves bump into building, hills, and other things as they travel, which can break up the signal. So tiny gaps are put between the 1s and 0s. As long as echoes from the buildings arrive in these gaps, the 1s and 0s will be received correctly by the digital radio, which then turns them into sound.

UNDERWATER SCOOTER

WHEN YOU GO SCUBA DIVING you have a limited amount of time underwater, which means you can't travel far before you need to resurface. Unless you have something to help you zip through the water—like an underwater scooter.

Scooters move quickly, but might scare fish into hiding!

Propellers

A propeller is a machine that moves a vehicle **forward** by pushing air or water **backward**. It has two or more twisted blades that stick out at an angle to a hub. The angle of the blade is called the **pitch**. As the blades turn, they push the water backward and the vehicle moves forward. Blades with a steep pitch make the vehicle go faster than blades with a shallow pitch.

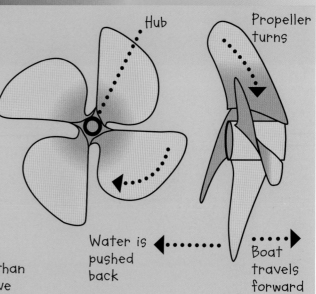

Hub

Propeller turns

Water is pushed back

Boat travels forward

Marine propellers are usually bigger and broader than airplane propellers because they don't have to move as quickly. Airplane propellers need to turn fast enough to stop the plane from falling out of the sky.

Airplane propeller

Boat propeller

Adding a twist to the blade makes the pitch change along its length. It is steepest near the hub and shallower at the tip. This makes the blade more efficient as it cuts through the water.

Diving bubble

Some scooters are equipped with a bubble-shaped helmet so that people can visit coral reefs or wrecks even if they can't scuba dive. Air is blown into the bubble to keep the water out and provide you with oxygen. (It's like turning a glass upside down in a bucket of water—at a certain point no more water will enter the glass.) You just put your head into the space and breathe!

ROBOTIC SUIT

UNTIL RECENTLY, wearable robots that give people superhuman strength were the stuff of science fiction. But such suits are now on sale in Japan. HAL-5, the most sophisticated yet, makes a person about five times stronger.

HAL-5 makes it easier to lift and carry heavy loads, such as these sacks of rice. The load is carried not just by the robotic arms but also by the legs, which flex at the hips and knees while also providing support.

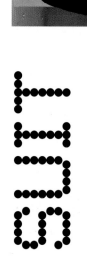

Powerful motors in the shoulders move the upper arms.

HAL-5 is an **"exoskeleton"** —a hard, external support frame like the external skeleton of an insect. Clamped tightly around the waist, arms, legs, and feet, it supports the whole body.

Battery pack

Control unit containing computer

How it works

HAL-5 works by **mirroring the body's own movement.** Sensors taped to the wearer's skin pick up the natural electrical signals sent from their brain to their muscles. These signals are relayed to a computer that activates powerful motors in the robot's arms and legs. Motion sensors make sure the motors don't move too much, which could injure the wearer or make him fall over.

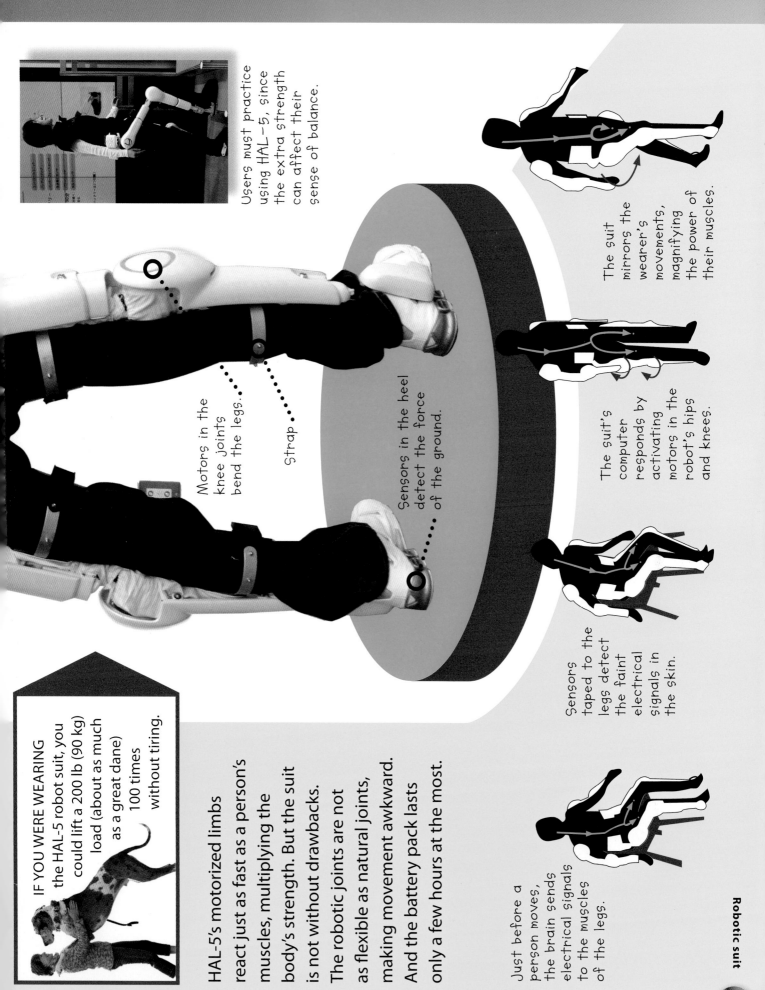

Users must practice using HAL-5, since the extra strength can affect their sense of balance.

Motors in the knee joints bend the legs.

Strap

Sensors in the heel detect the force of the ground.

IF YOU WERE WEARING the HAL-5 robot suit, you could lift a 200 lb (90 kg) load (about as much as a great dane) 100 times without tiring.

HAL-5's motorized limbs react just as fast as a person's muscles, multiplying the body's strength. But the suit is not without drawbacks. The robotic joints are not as flexible as natural joints, making movement awkward. And the battery pack lasts only a few hours at the most.

Just before a person moves, the brain sends electrical signals to the muscles of the legs.

Sensors taped to the legs detect the faint electrical signals in the skin.

The suit's computer responds by activating motors in the robot's hips and knees.

The suit mirrors the wearer's movements, magnifying the power of their muscles.

69

LIGHT GRAFFITI

DID YOU KNOW THAT YOU CAN DRAW PICTURES WITH A FLASHLIGHT? You wave it to draw your image in the air, then photograph the results. All you need is a camera and different colored lights.

Making light graffiti pictures uses a technique called **long-exposure photography.** This means leaving the shutter on the camera open for as long as possible so that it captures the movement of the light.

THE CAMERA is mounted on a tripod to keep it steady. The photographer-artist sets the exposure time and clicks the camera to open the shutter. Before it shuts, he or she quickly draws a picture using various colors of lights. The camera captures the movement of the light even though you can't see it happening.

Taking digital pictures

A camera's shutter controls how much light is let onto the sensor (or film in non-digital cameras). A shutter usually opens and closes in the blink of an eye, but you can set the **"exposure time"** on many cameras. This keeps the shutter open longer to take pictures in low light or to capture movement.

1 When you take a photograph, the shutter opens to allow light reflected off the scene to pass through the lens onto the sensor.

2 The sensor is covered in millions of tiny squares called pixels. These measure how much green, red, and blue light is shining on them and turns it into electrical signals.

3 The signals travel to the memory, where they are stored before being uploaded to a computer. The signals are then converted back into color on-screen.

Viewfinder

Light rays

Shutter

Sensor (or film)

Lenses

In the picture
Because the photographer-artist moves so fast, he often can't be seen in the picture or simply becomes a ghostly blur. If he wants to appear, he stands still for a few seconds before the shutter closes.

WIND TURBINES are simple machines. They consist of a gearbox, a generator, and several propeller blades set on top of a tall tower. Height is important—the wind moves faster the higher you are above the ground.

The blades on the world's biggest turbine measure 413 ft (126 m) from tip to tip. The blades are slightly curved to help them capture as much energy as possible from the wind.

When the wind is blowing hard enough, a typical turbine can produce enough electricity for a couple of thousand homes.

What's inside?

Wind-speed gauge

Gearbox

High-speed shaft

Controller

Generator

Brake

Low-speed shaft

The **wind** pushes the blades around. They are connected to a shaft that enters a **gearbox** full of **cogwheels**. The cogs increase the speed at which another shaft that leads to a generator is rotating. When the shaft is spinning fast enough, the **generator** starts to produce electricity.

WIND TURBINE

THERE IS ALWAYS A WIND BLOWING somewhere on Earth. Winds can be powerful and possess great energy. Turning that energy into something we can use requires a machine that can convert it into mechanical and then electrical energy. Such a machine is called a turbine.

You can fit around 100 people on each blade of a really big turbine.

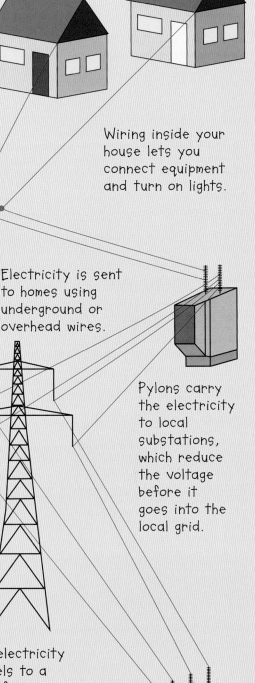

Wiring inside your house lets you connect equipment and turn on lights.

Electricity is sent to homes using underground or overhead wires.

Pylons carry the electricity to local substations, which reduce the voltage before it goes into the local grid.

The electricity travels to a transformer, which increases the voltage.

REFLECTIONS

REFLECTIONS ARE EVERYWHERE YOU LOOK. Without them, we wouldn't be able to see anything at all. Light is invisible until it bounces off something and enters our eyes. It doesn't bounce off all objects smoothly, but if it hits something shiny you get a perfect reflection.

WHEN YOU LOOK AT YOURSELF in a mirror you don't see yourself as other people see you. That is because a mirror flips the image back to front or left to right, like a printing block. Try holding this book up to a mirror and see what it does to the words. That's what it does to your face!

This is how you see yourself in a mirror.

This is how your friends see you.

Mirrors

Mirrors are flat pieces of glass that are coated with a layer of **shiny metal**, usually silver or aluminum. **A dark material** is put on the back to protect the metal. Light can travel through glass but not metal, so when it hits the smooth metal surface it **bounces** out again at the same angle. This forms the reflection that you see.

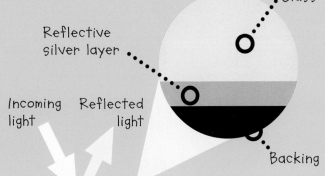

Glass

Reflective silver layer

Incoming light

Reflected light

Backing

If you put two mirrors opposite each other, you can get multiple reflections. This is because light bounces off one mirror and reflects it to the other. It then bounces a reflection back to the first mirror, and so on... until you have lots of ladies in red.

Concave mirrors

Curved surfaces have a different effect on reflections. When light hits a mirror that curves inward (concave), such as the bowl of a spoon, the rays are bent inward. If you're close to the mirror you will look larger. If you're farther away, you will appear smaller and upside down.

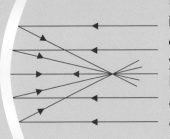

A concave mirror

Convex mirrors

Mirrors that curve outward are called convex mirrors. The back of a spoon is convex, so when you look at it you see yourself much smaller and also see more of the background around you. This is because the curved surface reflects the light rays outward.

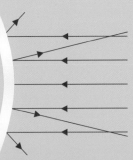

A convex mirror

LEVERS

IMAGINE YOU'VE GOT TO LIFT A BABY ELEPHANT OFF THE GROUND using only a long piece of wood and a couple of rocks. How do you do it? By making a lever (and hoping that the elephant behaves!).

What do levers do?

Levers are simple machines that increase or reduce a force (a push or pull movement). Lifting an elephant with a lever magnifies the force you supply, so you don't have to make as much effort. The simplest levers have a straight arm that turns on a fulcrum.

THE LONGER THE ARM IS, the more the force is increased at the other end. This means you can get more lift by moving the fulcrum closer to the thing you want to lift.

Force you apply

Fulcrum

Where you place the fulcrum makes a difference...

If the fulcrum is in the middle of the arm, then the force the lever produces will be the same as, or a bit more than, the force that is being applied at the other end.

If the force being applied is twice as far from the fulcrum as the other end of the arm, then the force at the other end will be twice as big.

Easy as one, two, three

There are three classes of levers:

CLASS ONE: The simplest levers, these include crowbars, seesaws, and scissors. The fulcrum is toward the middle. The force you apply at one end is usually increased at the other end.

Force you apply

Magnified force

Fulcrum

CLASS TWO: Wheelbarrows, nutcrackers, and garlic presses are typical class two levers. The fulcrum is at one end and you apply the force at the other, producing a much bigger force in the middle.

Force you apply

Fulcrum

Magnified force

CLASS THREE: These work the opposite way from class one and two levers, since they reduce the force you apply. This makes it easier to pick up small, delicate objects. Class three levers include tweezers, tongs, and chopsticks.

Fulcrum

Force you apply

Reduced force

Force from the lever

Your body is full of levers. Every time you pick something up, stand on tiptoe, or ride a bike, you are using levers.

If the force being applied is three times as far from the fulcrum as the other end of the arm, then the force at the other end will be three times as big.

GLOSSARY

3-D This stands for three-dimensional, which means that something has depth as well as height and width. You see a 3-D shape as it really is, rather than as a flat (2-D) shape.

Acceleration The rate at which a moving object speeds up.

Arc A section of a circle.

Atom The smallest part of an element that can exist on its own.

Buoyancy The ability of something to rise or float in a fluid of equal or greater density.

Carbonic acid A slightly acid liquid formed by dissolving carbon dioxide in water.

Charged particle A part of an atom that has a positive or negative electric charge.

Deceleration The rate at which a moving object slows down.

Density How much matter a particular material packs into a given space. This is affected by the size, mass, and number of atoms and how tightly they are packed together.

Digital Something that operates using a basic computer code of 1s and 0s.

Drag A force that slows an object down as it moves through the air or water.

Dynamo A machine that generates electricity.

Electromagnetic radiation The name given to energy waves, including radio, infrared, X-rays, and visible light.

Electron A tiny particle inside an atom that carries a negative electrical charge.

Element A substance made up of one kind of atom.

Evaporate To change from a liquid into a gas.

Flywheel A spinning wheel or disk that acts as a store of rotational energy.

Force A push or a pull.

Fulcrum The point that a lever turns on.

G-force The force exerted on anything that is accelerating or decelerating.

Gear A toothed wheel that connects with another toothed wheel. Gears are used to change the speed, force, or direction of a power source.

Glycerin A colorless, sweet liquid used to soften things.

Gravity A force that pulls objects toward each other. The pull from the center of Earth is what stops everything from floating into space.

Laser A device that produces a narrow beam of pure light.

Liquid crystal This is a substance that is midway between a solid and a liquid. This gives it unusual properties that are ideal for use in TV and computer screens and digital displays.

Magma Rock that has been heated underground until it is liquid.

Mass The amount of matter something has.

Matter The stuff that things are made from—atoms and molecules.

Molecule A group of atoms that are chemically joined together.

Morse code A system of dots and dashes used to represent letters and numbers. It was once used to send messages through telegraph wires, by radio, or by flashing lights.

Noble gas A chemical element that exists as a gas and does not react with other elements.

Pressure The amount of force pressing on each square meter of something.

Prism A piece of glass shaped to bend light through a particular angle.

Sap A liquid found in the stems of trees and plants.

Shock wave An intense wave of pressure caused by something moving faster than the speed of sound.

Supersonic Something that goes faster than the speed of sound in air (around 1,130 ft/s; 340 m/s).

Symmetry When an object can be reflected or rotated without looking any different.

Thrust A force that moves something forward.

Vapor Another word for gas.

Wavelength The distance from peak to peak or trough to trough of a wave.

INDEX

ACKNOWLEDGMENTS

The publisher would like to thank the following for their kind permission to reproduce their photographs:

(Key: a-above; b-below/bottom; c-center; f-far; l-left; r-right; t-top)

1 Science Photo Library: Martyn F. Chillmaid. **2 Alamy Images:** Ted Kinsman (b/soap film). **Dreamstime.com:** Andreus (tr); Jon Helgason (Klikk) (tl); Solarseven (cr). **3 Science Photo Library:** Ted Kinsman (r). **4 Alamy Images:** artpartner-images.com (ftl/bubble blower); Christopher Talbot Frank / Jaynes Gallery / Danita Delimont (tl/bubbles, ftr, cra/bubble, cr/bubbles). **5 Getty Images:** Richard Heeks / Barcroft Media . **6 Alamy Images:** Philip Quirk (main image). **Corbis:** Visuals Unlimited (tr). **7 Alamy Images:** Phil Degginger (clb). **Getty Images:** Ian Shive / Aurora (br). **8 Dreamstime.com:** Samum (cl); Igor Terekhov (Terex) (clb). **8–9 Science Photo Library:** Edward Kinsman (b/main image). **10 Dreamstime.com:** Sebastian Kaulitzki (Eraxion) (cla); Showface (b); Richard Thomas (Rtimages) (tr). **11 Dreamstime.com:** Showface (b). **12–13 Dreamstime.com:** Bee-nana (bubble background). **12 Dreamstime.com:** Alexirius (l). **13 Alamy Images:** Fred Hansen Photography / Bon Appétit (tr). **Dreamstime.com:** Showface (fbr). **14 MIT Media Lab:** (cr/electronic ink). **15 Alamy Images:** Martin Williams (tl). **Amazon.com, Inc.:** (tr). **CGTextures.com:** (bl). **Dreamstime.com:** Nikolai Tsvetkov (Koljambus) (bc). **16 Alamy Images:** Kolvenbach (bc); Maurice Savage (br). **16–17 Science Photo Library:** Gustoimages (x-ray image). **18 Dreamstime.com:** Dl1on (tr). **19 Corbis:** William Whitehurst (tr). **20–21 Alamy Images:** Pictor International / ImageState (main image).

20 Alamy Images: fotostox (bl). **22 Corbis:** Macduff Everton (bl). **Dreamstime.com:** Jon Helgason (Klikk) (tl). **23 Getty Images:** Howard Berman / The Image Bank . **24–25 Dreamstime.com:** Ryan Carter (Thisboy) (bursting balloon). **25 Alamy Images:** Martin Lee / mediablitzimages (UK) Limited (cr). **26 Alamy Images:** A. T. Willett . **27 Alamy Images:** A. T. Willett (tl, c, br). **28–29 BLOODHOUND SSC:** imaging by Siemens / Curventa (main car and background). **28 BLOODHOUND SSC:** imaging by Siemens / Curventa (cl). **Getty Images:** David Madison (cla). **29 BLOODHOUND SSC:** imaging by Siemens / Hywel Vaughan (tl, br). **Getty Images:** Dan Kitwood (fcr); Chris Ratcliffe / Bloomberg (cr). **30 Getty Images:** Chabruken (cl). **31 Science Photo Library:** Gustoimages. **32–33 Alamy Images:** AF Archive (film screen & audience). **32 Dreamstime.com:** Victor Zastol`skiy (Vicnt) (crb). **Science Photo Library:** Sovereign / ISM (bl/brain). **34 Fotolia:** Blueminiu (clb). **Science Photo Library:** Edward Kinsman (r). **36 Getty Images:** Time Life Pictures / Mansell (tc). **36–37 Corbis:** Mark Sykes / **Science Photo Library** (b). **37 Dreamstime.com:** Mishatc (clb). **38 Corbis:** Chaiwat Subprasom / Reuters. **39 Corbis:** Nicky Loh / Reuters (tl); Ocean (c). **40 Corbis:** Walter Geiersperger (l). **41 Dorling Kindersley:** Natural History Museum, London (fbl, bl/zircon, br/sapphire). **Fotolia:** Sebastian Kaulitzki (tr). **Science Photo Library:** Javier Trueba / MSF (tl). **42 Corbis:** Wayne Lynch / All Canada Photos (br). **Dreamstime.com:** Christopher Dodge (Christopherdodge) (clb/scan); Marcos2006 (tl). **43 Corbis:** Digital Art (cb). **Dreamstime.com:** Andreus (t); Winkyfish (clb); Sergiy Trofimov (Sergey76) (crb). **44–45 Dreamstime.com:** Nikolai Sorokin (Nikolais) (blue flying disc). **44 Aerobie, Inc. :** (bc). **Corbis:** Westend61 (clb). **46 Getty Images:** Laurent Gillieron / AFP (tl, br). **46–47 CGTextures.com:** (blue background). **Getty Images:** Fabrice Coffrini / AFP (main image). **47 Alamy Images:** Finnbarr Webster (bc).

Science Photo Library: Eye of Science (tl). **48 Science Photo Library:** Glphotostock (ca). **48–49 Corbis:** Karl Weatherly (main image and background). **49 All Rights Reserved © tomgamache.com:** (clb). **51 Dreamstime.com:** Jeffrey Banke (Jeffbanke) (deer). **Science Photo Library:** (br). **52 Science Photo Library:** Gustoimages (br). **53 Dreamstime.com:** Py2000 (tr). **Science Photo Library:** Gustoimages (br, bl). **54 Alamy Images:** Jeremy Sutton-Hibbert (bl); Chris Willson (cl). **54–55 Science Photo Library:** Gustoimages (main image). **56 Corbis:** John Gillmoure (tr); Antonio M. Rosario / Tetra Images (l). **Science Photo Library:** Sinclair Stammers (crb). **56–57 Corbis:** Layne Kennedy (cb). **57 Dreamstime.com:** Michael Ludwig (Diver721) (crb); Maryna Melnyk (P6m5) (cra); Solarseven (cr). **Science Photo Library:** (bc); Gregory Sams (main image). **58–59 Corbis:** Paul Freytag (main image). **60 Dreamstime.com:** Dmytro Kozlov (Amid) (clb). **Science Photo Library:** Kenneth Libbrecht (tr). **60–61 Science Photo Library:** Kenneth Libbrecht (largest flake). **61 Science Photo Library:** Ted Kinsman (cr); Kenneth Libbrecht (tl, fbl, ca, bc, ftr, cra, br). **62 Image courtesy of FLIR Systems:** (br). **Science Photo Library:** Tony McConnell (cla). **63 Science Photo Library:** Tony McConnell. **64–65 Science Photo Library:** Mehau Kulyk (radio masts and waves). **65 Science Photo Library:** Friedrich Saurer (cra/wavelengths diagram). **66 Corbis:** Stephen Frink. **67 Alamy Images:** Stephen Frink Collection (br). **Dreamstime.com:** Yury Shirokov (Yuris) (cl). **Getty Images:** Cavan Images / The Image Bank (fcl). **68 Corbis:** Kimimasa Mayama / Reuters (cla). **68–69 Rex Features:** Sutton-Hibbert (main image). **69 Corbis:** Ocean (bl). **Rex Features:** News Pictures / MCP (tl). **70–71 Rex Features:** Marc Cameron / Mark Brown (b/main image). **70 Dreamstime.com:** Artur Synenko (Connect1) ftl, tr/; Paul Vinten (Paulvinten) (bl). **Rex Features:** Michael Bosanko / Talk Talk (tl).

71 Dreamstime.com: Christopher King (Wingnutdesigns); (cla); Steve2009 (cr). **Rex Features:** Michael Bosanko / Talk Talk (br). **72–73 Alamy Images:** Simon Belcher (main image). **74–75 Corbis:** Holger Hollemann / EPA (main image). **74 Corbis:** Jesse Kuhn / Illustration Works (bl). **75 Science Photo Library:** Andrew Lambert Photography (cr, crb). **76 Dreamstime.com:** Andersastphoto (clb); Kostyantin Pankin (Vipdesignusa) tl; Olivier Le Queinec (Olivierl) (crb). **76–77 Dreamstime.com:** Andersastphoto (b/rock on lever). **77 Dreamstime.com:** Carlos Caetano (Ccaetano) (crb); Denise Campione (Zeneece) (br). **78–79 Corbis:** Ocean (bubbles). **78 Getty Images:** Huw Jones / Liquid / Nonstock (bl). **80 Corbis:** John Gillmoure (t/frost, b/frost). **Science Photo Library:** Kenneth Libbrecht (cra, bl, clb, br, fcra, fbr, tr, fcra/hexagonal snowflake, ftl/hexagonal snowflake, ftl).

Jacket images: Getty Images: Rick Lew b; Front: **Science Photo Library:** Gustoimages (robot dog); Back: **Alamy Images:** Christopher Talbot Frank / Jaynes Gallery / Danita Delimont, cl, fclb, clb, tl; **Science Photo Library:** Claire Deprez / Reporters br/ (wind turbines), Gustoimages tr.

All other images © Dorling Kindersley For further information see: www.dkimages.com